This is What Life Does

This is What Life Does

Poetry by

Anne Randolph

© 2022 Anne Randolph. All rights reserved.
This material may not be reproduced in any form, published,
reprinted, recorded, performed, broadcast,
rewritten or redistributed without
the explicit permission of Anne Randolph.
All such actions are strictly prohibited by law.

Cover design by Shay Culligan
Cover photo by Anne Randolph

ISBN: 978-1-63980-211-1

Kelsay Books
502 South 1040 East, A-119
American Fork, Utah 84003
Kelsaybooks.com

for Jim, with eternal gratitude

Acknowledgements

Grateful acknowledgement is made to the editors of these journals, where several of the poems appeared, some slightly altered:

Cloudbank: "First Sign of Spring," "A Gardener's Life," "Late at Night," "Winter Solstice 2020, Ohio"

The Flint Hills Review: "In Late Afternoon"

Iconoclast: "1797, Miracle Year," "When Wordsworth Wrote in a Frenzy"

The Listening Eye: "Climbing the Peaks, England," "How Do You Write a Letter"

Mock Turtle Zine: "This is What Life Does," "First Trip to Cleveland" (best of show, Dayton Metro Library Poetry Contest, 2014), "The Unearthing" (Dayton Metro Library prize Winner), "Village News," "Women's Park, Yellow Springs, Ohio"

Snowy Egret: "Garden Gifts," "The Hummingbird in My Garage," "Into the Wild," "Firefly Festival," "Any Common Loss," "Hiking Near Buttermere, England"

Tiny Seed Literary Journal: "Bird Intrigue"

Yellow Springs News: "Mary's Garden"

Contents

I. This is what life does

This is what life does	15
Valentine rewind	17
First trip to Cleveland	18
Nesting	20
Courtship on the Kamelands trail	21
Power down	23

II. A gardener's life

First sign of spring	27
Phoenix rising	28
This morning I stay inside	29
Bird intrigue	30
Garden gifts	31
A gardener's life	32
Manfred the mantis	34
July surprise	35
The hummingbird in my garage	36
The unearthing	37
In late summer	38
Journey to solstice	39

III. Into the wild

Forest bathing in spring	43
Into the wild	44
Firefly festival	45
Our mountain	46
Late at night	47
Any common loss	48
Focusing on the planets	49
Winter solstice 2020, Ohio	50

IV. Climbing the peaks, England

Climbing the peaks, England	53
Hiking near Buttermere, England	54
Encounter on an English footpath	55
Sheep herding in the Lake District	56
Trying to find the hunting tower	57
1797, miracle year	58
When Wordsworth wrote in a frenzy	59

V. Village news

Village news	63
How do you write a letter	64
Front porch sanctuary	65
Missing you	66
Mary's garden	67
Women's Park, Yellow Springs, Ohio	68

I. This is what life does

This is what life does

This is what life does. It takes you
to a conference at an arboretum where
you sit in back so you can stare out
the window at trees and birds at their
feeders. When people start introducing
themselves, life lets you remember
the guy who stands up in front,
the one who last whispered
good night to you forty years
ago. Then it gives you courage
to seek him at the coffee break
so you can hear him say *I've always
wondered what happened to you.*
But it's under trees over lunch
that life lets you pick up loose
threads, patch the gaps, and stitch
a fresh connection. And then,
life makes you wait some more.

Out of the blue, a phone call,
an invitation to spend a day at the family
cottage on a lake. There is no hesitation
in your answer. Armed with poems,
sandwiches and soup, you follow
the curving string of a country road
on a treasure hunt. Lakeside vacation
homes cram the lanes until you cross
a bridge to find a quaint cottage on
a point. There, life lets you breathe.

A day of canoeing, poetry, song and
conversation. You smile when he edges
closer to see photos on your camera. And when
you are ready to leave, you feel fire
burning in his sparkling eyes,
his body trembling to hold you.

Valentine rewind

The week after Valentine's Day my lover
gives me red-orange tulips—*a new poem,*
he jokes. They are wrapped in crisp
cellophane that makes crackling sounds.
White strings tie around straight
stems. I place them in a tall clear
vase on the dining table where they begin
to relax in warm light. Buds open
in the steam of salmon chowder
for supper. Yellow tulip centers hang
like red rimmed suns over our heads,
as he inches his chair close to mine.

First trip to Cleveland

We start out as if on a lark, a romantic getaway
north to lake country, whipping by Amish
fields of straw sheaves, lined up like skirted
scarecrows, then that city skyline,
so jagged and uneven, a mouth with
missing teeth. Our bed and breakfast,
a stone mansion from grander days,
rock 'n roll guitar sculpture marking the entrance.

Hurrying, we walk to the museum before closing,
meet Bonnard's wife Marthe, feel the dappling
sun of Renoir, and search in vain for prints,
watercolors, all stowed in dark archives,
available by appointment. At dinner
we share everything, conversation, laughter,
an artichoke trimmed and dressed
in lemon, chicken breasts creamed
with goat cheese. Back at the inn, you study
your books while the woman next door coughs
erratically. We move into a new room,
where we rest under a blinking
smoke alarm, awakened in the early
morning by the repeated clearing of a throat.

At the clinic, you lug your heavy bag
of hope to all three doctors, search for
answers, as I record conversations, no cracks
in the door to alternative treatments, only
surgery or radiation, the implanting
of seeds on a seek and destroy mission,

titanium husks you would always
carry deep inside, like a portable
landfill in a scarred landscape. Afterwards,
I drive us south, now and then stroking
the softness of your grey corduroys, silence
our companion the whole way home.

Nesting

Two large cushions at the back
of my sofa lean toward each other
like my grandmother and great-aunt
when in conversation years ago,
adjusting hearing aids,
one lifting an arm expressively,
both in rapt attention, straining to listen.

Reupholstered in a yellow vining brocade,
the couch now rests in my computer room.
Sometimes small white feather ends stick out
of the fabric, gently pricking skin. When my partner
and I sit down to watch movies on the screen,
we tilt toward the middle, two love birds
in a feathered nest. Occasionally one of us
asks the other to repeat what we've heard,
turning up the volume so we don't miss a word.

Courtship on the Kamelands trail

We enter a cattle tunnel under a highway,
the old farm long abandoned,
now a nature preserve, the pasture invaded
by cedars and silvery autumn olives.
Beavers have felled skinny trees to build a dam,
creating an algae-covered pond. Decked
with binoculars and backpacks, my partner
and I are on a mission to discover migratory birds.

The trail leads into a woods full of song—
a chorus raining down from treetops.
In the lead, I step quietly as a stalking cat.
A pair of red-brown thrashers, speckled
breasts, come into focus on a downed log.
They look at each other, then run down
the bark, the male chasing the female
in the old game.

In a small clearing we spot a pair of red-headed
woodpeckers, clad in their black and white
tuxedoes, hoods like plush red-velvet.
Flying quickly from tree to tree, they
puncture the air with shrill calls, bob heads
at each other, in full courtship mode.
We are surprised when they perch on opposite
sides of a tree trunk, hop around until
they spy each other, then instantly duck
out of sight, only to repeat their game
of hide and seek, like excited children.

As I wander ahead, I hear a *chick-burr,
chick-burr,* look up to behold a scarlet
tanager, bedecked in flaming red with
black wings. He seems to be calling to me
and flies closer. I am motionless, silent
as stone. As his image sharpens, I admire
his thick yellowish beak in brief moments
of communion.

Suddenly, my mate whistles our secret code,
come see, come see!

Power down

I was rinsing the last dinner dish.
Lights sputtered, then blackness.
You exclaimed *I'll get my flashlight!*
As I stepped across the floor,
groping for my phone, I shouted
Don't move!

Opening a curtain, we gasped at black
house silhouettes against a town-lit sky.
Found our way to a closet, clutched
pink and green lamps and tall
shell-crusted candles. Scattered them
around the hallway and living room,
like Halloween torches in a haunted house.

As the temperature dropped, we donned
down vests, huddled close on the orange couch,
shared tiny reading lights arcing over
open books. Started a crossword puzzle,
clues pulling memories of favorite
children's stories, the Munch Museum,
and an Oregon estuary.

We hardly noticed when all the lights
blazed on. We were tracing a constellation
created by the puzzle's x's,
little dipper arising from under
our fingers.

II. A gardener's life

First sign of spring

My next-door neighbor Peggy texts
me, *Spring has sprung—I see your
mower man coming—a beautiful sight!*
A smile spreads over my face.
The fellow comes each year to mow
scraggy remnants of my wildflower
meadow—withered empty seed heads
of grey coreopsis, dried grasses
and straw stalks of goldenrod.

The mower man scours the land,
searching for standing water before
revving his engine. I join him,
my feet sinking into soil's softness.
The hum of his machine brings summer's
comfort to a cold March day.
A glorious sound! Peggy texts.

Meadow is a verb in a Native American
language. New life stirs beneath
winter soil—roots of purple coneflower,
blazing star, butterfly weed
and prairie dropseed soon to propel
the first slender green leaves.
A tender journey to summer's
yellow, orange and purple
waving in the breeze
at Peggy and me.

Phoenix rising

In early June, when serviceberry's branches
are heavy with fruit, cedar waxwings arrow
into our tree to feed. Before opening a window, I pause,
captivated by a male and female passing a berry back and forth,
from bill to bill, until the female swallows it.

One day six waxwings fly in. Startled
by something, they flee toward the house.
To our horror, one crashes into the dining room window.
We press our faces to the glass, see him lying
still on the grass, strain to see if he is still breathing.
His waxy red wing tips splay, tail feather tipped bright yellow.

We hover over him near the window and pray.
When a few ants creep over his body, we fear the worst.
Suddenly, as if tickled, the bird vigorously shakes
his head and tail feathers, rises and smoothly
soars straight to the nearest tall tree.
We shout with joy, clap our hands and give thanks,
hoping he isn't injured, and can find his mate,
who didn't wait.

This morning I stay inside

so I do not break the flight
of bluebirds flitting from fence to grass
and up again in my backyard,
nor interrupt purple finches gathered
round the bird bath, drinking
and splashing, or halt hummingbirds
sipping red flutes of pineapple sage.

The sun blazes yellow and burnt orange
leaves of the young smoke tree, which shall not
see my shadow. A monarch butterfly waves
stained glass wings, alights on goldenrod
growing in the wild strip beyond my garden.
Only bees to bother him.

And I at my window, binoculars in hand,
await with suspended breath the next movement
of this silent symphony, this astonishing dance.

Bird intrigue

After my burgundy and yellow zinnias burst
into bloom, goldfinches grasp stems to pluck
petals, one by one, *"she loves me, she loves
me not."* When I spy the marauders denuding
flowers planted to attract butterflies, I dash out
the back door, scattering birds to the sky.
They tweet their alarm, *"oh you, oh you!"*

I cannot fathom a reason for their destruction,
patrol the garden periodically, prepared
to defend my beauties, visited
by nectaring tiger and zebra swallowtails.
I clip damaged pocked heads, but the finches move
on to the next flowers, continuing their pecking.

One day from a window, I discover
what the birds are seeking, watch them yank
wispy seeds with their beaks and swallow.
I stop chasing the thieves, let bare
flowers remain. As I pull a flimsy strand
from a tight rust-colored head, I find
at the end a shiny white transparent sheath,
shaped like a shield, encasing a tiny dark seed,
spirit food for butterflies, bees and birds.

Garden gifts

When a ruby-throated hummingbird
flashes iridescent green against
red flutes of cardinal flowers,

when yellow-striped black wings of a giant
swallowtail flutter over the small
button of a pink zinnia,

when a dragonfly's blue and lacy black
wings land on my shoulder as I water
wildflowers,

my breath stills. Like rising monarchs
fanning each other, dancing to sky
in a rippling column of orange,
spirit soars.

A gardener's life

When she was young, she lived within
the rustle of underbrush, imagining
rooms, or just hiding from boys.
There, under a neighbor's shrub,
she found a tree seedling struggling
in darkness, dug it up, and transplanted
it to her backyard, where she watched
it grow as she grew, then shoot past her.

One summer, she daily drenched
a watermelon plant with devotion.
The heaviness of the watering can,
carrying it down the long yard,
did not defeat her. A ball grew slowly,
inflating itself into unimaginable sweetness,
a fleeting reward for her pains.

Herbs became her passion when
her children were young. Vanilla
scent of dried sweet woodruff
perfumed the air. She cut
hollow stems of celery-flavored
lovage for her kids' tomato juice.
After lavender budded, they harvested it,
sat on the back porch and wove
thin ribbons around bent stems, encasing
the blooms, creating wands.

Later, nest empty, she moved to a small
house with a wild strip for a back yard.
Filled it with purple coneflowers,
blazing stars and tall coreopsis,
enticing bees, butterflies and birds.

Watched life return to her in the seesaw
of goldfinch swinging from seed heads,
singing as they swayed.

Now, no longer able to wield a shovel,
she hires a young worker to put in new plants.
Spends the winter deciding what to add next,
stews over color combinations, rare
and endangered native species.
She's still watching her garden grow,
as she grows, now over ninety seasons,
renewing the wildness in her
one more time.

Manfred the mantis

My friend plucks her praying mantis
off his terrarium wall, places his leafy
green folded body on my open palm.
His tiny feet like suction cups
on my skin, gently squeezing.
When I speak, he rotates his triangular
head to stare at me with Martian eyes.
A shiver rolls down my back.
His forelegs finger shiny yarns
of my sweater sleeve.

He likes resting on my friend's hand;
spellbound, they watch *Nature* on TV.
Sometimes he walks up her arm,
pauses at her shoulder to stroke
her fine blond hair, then inches
over to pat her cheek.

July surprise

Camera in hand, I stand along
my back yard's wild strip,
admire lavender bee balm,
pink liatris stalks and dainty
red stars of cardinal flowers.
Skittish monarchs flit to and fro,
little orange kites sailing
on breezes.

Like a gift, a giant swallowtail swoops
into the back of the garden, raised wings
blazing two yellow V's on black.
I wait for him to come closer for a photo,
but there are so many bee balms.
Holding still as a tree, I barely breathe.
Minutes pass as I watch him,
but he never moves nearer.

Then, in a flash, he lands
on a flower not more than a foot away.
I am stunned as he unfolds
and flattens his great wings,
yellow lines transforming
into two strands of golden teeth,
shaping a gaping smile.

The hummingbird in my garage

zooms wildly along the stucco ceiling,
trying to break through a crusty cloud.
Garage door open, he never swoops low
enough to escape. Occasionally he rests
on a high wire, like an acrobat.

I plant a sprinkler sculpture in a bucket full
of mulch and hang a red feeder.
Opening a small door, I close the other,
as he continues to peck at the ceiling.
With an upended broom, I try to whisk
him out, but he ignores guidance.
I fret I might accidentally
touch his wings.

I stand still as a tree, broom like
a straight branch. In seconds,
he alights on the straw ends. Slowly,
I walk with him, like an acolyte
carrying a cross. Lowering my burden,
I maneuver him through the door.
My heart flutters as he blinks
for a few seconds,
then flies.

The unearthing

I pick up a pink granite rock, one side flat,
slip my fingers into faint fingerholds.
A Woodland Indian village once
stretched across my subdivision.
Each time a new home site is excavated, bulldozers
heap hills of soil and rock, like burial mounds.
I scour turned soil for relics, spot speckled
green and pink granite stones, wash them off,
try to figure out their function—grinding,
polishing, pecking or hammering.

Lining my collection across the kitchen counter,
I grasp a smooth long hammerstone,
imagine it smashing nuts, grains or roots.
I wonder what scents arose from
grains like goosefoot ground for porridge or bread.
Although ancient Indian recipes are lost,
these stone survivors of disease and war keep
a link to tribal women, the work around fires,
as if my hand touches theirs when I cradle them.

In late summer

wind sweeps the trees, bends branches back
like ocean waves.
The whitish undersides of leaves display.
Breezes build into a roaring chorus
that crashes over purple asters and goldenrod,
bobbing in all directions, holding fast to earth
like seaweed clings to rocks.

Wispy skirted seeds of butterfly weed float by
like sea foam, followed by clanging chimes.
I am gliding, my bench
a boat, sailing among the swells.

Journey to solstice

It is the thin time of the year
when daylight is squeezed, like sand
in the narrow part of an hourglass.

The sun hugs the southern sky,
spreading the trees' long shadows,
moving slowly, like hands
on a clock.

I stand on the edge of mid-December
and peer at the pool of approaching
holidays, the whorls and eddies
soon to catch me in their flow.

I will feel the pinch
of those narrower days to come,
and amid increasing frenzy, pause,
to remember January, the stretching out
of empty days blank as snow,
growing in light, in beginnings.

III. Into the wild

Forest bathing in spring

Late afternoon light warms the hillside
between striped shadows of trees.
I walk hesitantly, new at this exercise
in the woods, without destination.
Breezes blow spicebush branches
sprouting tender lime-green leaves
as tiny insects catch the sun in a dizzying
mid-air waltz. I break the spell,
bend to pull invasive white-flowered
garlic mustard. How easily the tall
smooth stems release their small root
from rich soil, like candles from cake.
How hard to remove myself from
temptation of task.

After hanging bare-rooted weeds in forks
of trees, I refocus on what is moving.
Tall golden ragworts burst forth tiny
daisies, like sprays of fireworks.
A huge beech tree lies along a valley
floor, its beautiful bark beckoning.
My feet snap branches as I make
my way slowly down a hill.

I find a place to sit in shade on smooth
wrinkled bark. There seems little left
to notice in the great green silence.
A hint of dark purple suddenly catches
my eye. Rare dwarf larkspur springs
into view, blue violet dye blooming
in dark patches over the hillside.
Buds the shape of dolphins swimming
in air.

Into the wild

A young girl claims an overgrown area
wedged between green lawns
and manicured bushes, where tree branches arc
and curving limbs of honeysuckle splay,
creating small rooms.

She sweeps out sticks and rocks, cuts
a neighbor's rhubarb leaves for rugs, pushes
broken branches into place for benches.
On the rope of a swinging grapevine
she happily bounces her small frame.
Her Labrador rolls side to side on cool earth.
Squeezing her eyes closed, she commands
her mind to remember this moment, the smell
of dry leaves, roughness of grapevine,
dog panting in the heat, tail beating the earth
like a drum.

Many years later a grey-haired woman on a walk
discovers a small tangled woods between two
homes in her new neighborhood. She smiles
as a memory flashes, feels pulled to crawl beneath boughs.

Firefly festival

On the last evening of a firefly course,
we carpool south to an Adams county
flood plain, scent of mowed paths
between tall ironweed under a clouded moon.
Chirping tree toads, crickets and cicadas,
shaking their tambourines, compose the night chorus.

Big dippers blink, fly in j patterns
at dusk while small greys wink like
tiny holiday lights strung in bushes.
All this to attract females,
who lie in wait for the right
blinking pattern, then turn their
abdomens towards the chosen one,
flashing an invitation.

Chinese lantern fireflies we seek
have moved to tops of trees.
We strain to see their slow glows,
spy a streaking yellow-green
flame as it sears the black fabric of night.

Our mountain

A two-story heap of excavated soil
from a new home-site rests
in the middle of my development.
On windy days the dirt dusts
back porch furniture, sticks to screens.
Neighborhood children climb
to the peak, throw balls and toys,
slide down worn paths, push bikes
to the top.

One night, the hill hosted a runaway child,
armed with just a flashlight, until,
cold and hungry, he was coaxed
down by a neighbor offering
a peanut butter sandwich.

This summer it has softened
with plant growth, like an old
Appalachian mountain gently
settled in place. At twilight,
queen anne's lace, glowing
all around the base, holds the hill aloft
as evening shadows gather.
Swallows take to the air,
dart and dash, up and around
our mountain, where neighbors meet
to watch the moon rise.

Late at night

eerie sounds seep through
my living room windows,
crescendo like laments from
the dead. Curious, I slide open
the back porch door and step
into a cacophony of coyotes
in a field nearby, wailing like
sirens, crowing like roosters,
yipping, howling, whining
and barking like dogs, a dissonant
choir that never pulls together.
I cringe at the unholy cries.

Concluding nearly as quickly as it arose,
the frenzy fades and quiet is restored—
the night returned to crickets,
katydids and grasshoppers,
the rhythm and repetition of their
cheerful chirps and songs in sync
with the beating of my heart.

And yet, I yearn for my own
wild tribe.

Any common loss

takes me into the woods,
where I sit next to an Indian burial mound
from 500 BC and gaze up at red-orange
leaves of oak trees dancing against a sky
so blue I could swim in it. A hawk turns
around a pillar of air, over and over,
its white underside lit by the sun.

The air smells as rich and sweet as cider.
Just breathing it feeds some part of me.
Suddenly a fat lime-green bug flies
by my face, a tiny airship, crashing into
a clump of leaves. A woodpecker
hammers away in the distance. Squirrels
chatter and my desolation drains into
the mound, as life has its way with loss,
brown leaves turning into a lushness
only time can deliver.

Focusing on the planets

Our friend's night telescope is wheeled
onto blacktop. Like a small cannon,
its barrel points up, as if ready to blast the stars.
We take turns peering through the eyepiece—
first at Jupiter, its bands of grey gaseous clouds
shrouding mystery. Two of its moons
close together, like white marbles.
We switch to nearby Saturn, cast in a hard light,
rings merged in a thick bright circle,
like a life saver mint.

The planets shift behind trees as we spin
with the earth. When the telescope is turned
to the crescent moon, I exclaim over
its closeness and clarity, as if I could
touch its brown crusty surface pocked
with craters. Where its curving edge meets darkness,
stark silhouettes of hills and mountains rise,
as if ready to flake off into the depths.
Only one side of the moon's face is ever seen,
its hidden obscurity like a shadow
we might carry.

Winter solstice 2020, Ohio

The solstice arrives dressed in dark grey,
day slipping away like a thief.
In frosty air of evening, I let darkness
hold me, dissolve into night.
Like secret lovers, the great conjunction
occurs behind a curtain of clouds. Jupiter
and Saturn, traveling two sides
of a V-formation like migratory geese,
are merging into a spectacular white star,
sharing rings.

I crave to be on a Kansas plain, where the night sky
is clear, speckled with thousands of winking lights,
where I could raise my hand to the brilliant
convergence, spark the star on my ring finger,
marry the night.

# IV. Climbing the peaks, England

IV Climbing the rocks: England

Climbing the peaks, England

Pointed out by the local grocer,
the street evolves into a public footpath.
We ascend past medieval drystone walls,
layered with lichens and moss,
enclosing pasture for sheep or cattle.
Small holes formed by fence builders
give passage to hares, voles, and hedgehogs.
Each step taken imprints ancestral
memory. Did they pass this way?

Patches of pink-lavender heather
still bloom against silver crusted rock.
Abandoned millstones from another age
are cast aside like wagon wheels.
Longhorn cattle in shaggy coats graze,
oblivious. At the peak, a jagged gritstone edge
rises over a verdant valley,
sprinkled with tiny villages.

Space opens out all around us,
from rocky plateau to valley,
hills and heathered moors.
We are like trees catching the wind.
Roots surge, spreading into the landscape,
like joy.

Hiking near Buttermere, England

We climb a mountain carpeted with grassy
trails and rust-colored bracken ferns.
Footholds are rounded indentations made by generations
of grazing sheep. Scattered over the hillsides
like clumps of snow, they watch us with wary eyes.
I stretch my hand to touch a curly wooly
head, but the sheep quickly steps away.
On our descent we find a few resting next
to a 17th century stone church on a slope
outside the village—posing for a flock
of photographers.

Later in the week, hiking around a sparkling blue lake
reflecting clouds, we come upon a sign that states in bold:
"Worrying Sheep is an Offense." At the end of the trail,
dusk settling in, we pass a cottage, a trailer parked nearby
holding four of the fleecy animals. Stench of manure.
I speak softly to them while they watch us go by.
When we reach the rear, they stampede to the door.
I want to unlatch it, let them bolt to the hillsides.

Encounter on an English footpath

Passing by a pasture, we spot a black-faced sheep.
He runs up to us on his side of the fence, like an old friend,
stares pleadingly, then bleats loudly over
and over, jumping side to side as if in a panic.
We try to calm him with soothing assurances,
but are helpless. Where is his flock?

We walk on, and he trots alongside us for a spell,
as if we are leading him where he wants
to go. Then he leaps away. Finally, we reach
the shepherd, who reunites the stray
with his flock.

The fright he felt when separated, something
we couldn't forget, like my sister's Lab
the day she was lost downtown, dashing
to the driver's window of each car at the light
to see if my sister was inside.

Sheep herding in the Lake District

One morning, feasting on sausage and eggs next
to our hotel's bay window, we are surprised

by a tremendous beating sound on the street outside.
A wave of sheep pours past, herded by sheep dogs,

and shepherds on ATV's, hatless in driving rain.
Grim determination on their faces as they

block off streets, narrowly avoiding tourists.
A quick hand signal from one shepherd sends dogs

bounding up a hill to search for stragglers. All are evicted
from a churchyard by the snarling, yipping black and white
demons.

Trying to find the hunting tower

on this grand estate, we ask hikers for directions.
From an endless road, we enter a trail
through woods, climb past green
moss-covered boulders like sentient beings.
Hopelessly lost again, we trudge on.
Around a corner, splashing sounds of a waterfall.
Closer, we spy three generations enjoying lunch,
huddled together on stone steps near the falls.
Shouting above the roar, we ask the way to the Tower.
"Off to the left on the road above,"
booms the grandfather, with heavy British accent
between bites of sandwich.
We gingerly ascend the steps
between them.

Suddenly a boy exclaims over
a fuzzy brown-striped caterpillar wending
its way over a broad rock face. My partner asserts
"We have those in America!"
The grandmother shoots back "And
I suppose they're *bigger* there!"

1797, miracle year

At a field gate, after miles of walking,
Coleridge spots Wordsworth and his sister
working in their garden. Like a colt,
he crashes through corn to reach them.
A joyful meeting ensues as he recounts
a black rook creaking overhead
as it led him through purple heath
flowers and yellow-lit groves.

For weeks they ramble the Quantuck hills, feeding
their writing from images of lakes, fields, forests and ocean.
Lines from Dorothy's journal inspire: *withered holly
leaves dancing with a hailstorm* and
daffodils laughing with the wind.

In the months that follow, they write
at the same table, one man's lines leaking
into stanzas written by the other, as they sketch
the outline of a new ballad about a terrible curse
caused by the killing of an albatross.

When Wordsworth wrote in a frenzy

of feeling, birthing pains crept up his
left side. Beset, he collapsed into bed.
His wife's excuse: *he labors
with a sonnet.* Once a poem was
born, his sister Dorothy nursed
the newborn onto a white page.

In less fevered times, walking spawned
his writing. At home he trod up
and down a straight gravel path,
stones crunching beneath boots, air
heavy with the oily scent of damp sheep.
Hundreds of lines erupted over time
as he walked his way inward.

Dorothy, sister of his soul, breathed
words that found their way into
his poems—her childhood fear
of brushing the dust off a butterfly's wings.
Lying on grass side by side, gazing
at the clear night sky, they saw
their reflection in Gemini, the twins,
holding hands in eternal flickering light.

V. Village news

Village news

Lately, at any given glance of the newspaper,
the shock, kick in the stomach, at who we
have suddenly lost. Last week, Annemone
from Germany, who died while watering
her garden, who liked to bake cherry
and plum tortes with fruit from her trees.

Now Brian, a sculptor of renown, who never
knew a stranger, famous for his glittering
blue eyes, easy, wide smile, always entreating
me when downtown with *let's all get together
for dinner.* Once his outrageous flirtation
with the pretty postal clerk made me laugh
inside, as I stood in line.

He and Marie loved shaking their booties
to Friday night music at the cafe.
Like a hungry thief, death devoured him
before he completed a sculpture of a former slave
turned landowner, giver of property
for our village park.

A greeting from a friend or acquaintance
in a theater or grocery line, a conversation across
a restaurant table, or on the street, could be the last,
each fleeting moment of interaction
dusted with gold.

How do you write a letter

to someone who is dying too young,
just weeks left, seconds slipping by
like water in a stream? A champion
of African rhino preservation, teacher
of conservation to children, national
park ranger and leader of weekend
birding workshops, he left parts
of himself all over the world.

Birding with him was like stepping
into an exotic universe as the black-
billed cuckoo called to us in Ohio woods,
among a multitude of yellow warblers.
He identified all the different languages,
as we strained our eyes along river bluffs
and prairie meadows. Our joy when
we could name the birds by their sound.

Perhaps he would like to know about
the two doves in my backyard who seem
to be kissing or preening each other
in rapid back and forth movements.
When they arch their necks to peck
their fluffy backs, their eyes close into
light blue discs against grey.

Now he teaches us in his waltz with
death, the exhaustion of the dance,
in his acceptance and peace about
what is to come, windows open
to the flute of the wood thrush
floating through the forest,
calling him.

Front porch sanctuary

She would carefully cut, then lift
leafy branches while they were feasting.
Place them in a tall wire cage topped
with a net on her front porch.
So many yellow and black striped bodies,
their only thought to munch
as many milkweed leaves as possible.
Ballooning in just a few days,
they magically morphed into chrysalises.
Delicate pale green cases dotted with gold.

Her lovely photo arrived on my phone—
"Here's our hatch today!"
Two wet orange and black Monarchs
hung like ornaments.
She carried branches to a butterfly
bush so wings could dry in sun.
Later they fluttered around
fluffy pink blooms, nectaring.

So many butterflies burst forth
that last summer, offering
over and over the possibility
of transcendence,
like a promise.

Missing you

in memory of Mary

Today when I deleted all my voicemail
messages, I didn't realize what I was doing.
Later a neighbor came by, said you were
in hospice. My stomach dropped.
Then the repeated *I can't believe it.*

Just two weeks ago I saw you at the movies.
You radiated how glad you were
to be in remission, as we grasped each other's arms.
Next day you sent me
the Stafford poem about finding
his muse, how he took her hand.
I won't be able to take yours again.

I left you one last voicemail
before my voice cracked.
All I could offer, my prayers and love.
I undeleted all your messages,
saved your gentle laugh.

Mary's garden

After a harvest, she blended basil with water,
poured the puree into ice cube trays for freezing.
When I prepared to leave with my fresh treasure,
she pressed a bag of frozen green squares
into my hand.

Now it is winter, and suddenly she is gone.

I pull the cubes she gave me out of the freezer,
plop them in soup. As they melt in a green swirl,
we are working in her garden, bees buzzing,
cutting off buds and flowers, forcing new growth.
The pungent fragrance, like licorice, seeps
into our fingers, perfumes the air.
Flushed and excited in the intense heat,
we share stories and much laughter.

She was the sun,
and I basked in her light.

Women's Park, Yellow Springs, Ohio

The serpentine red brick path unfurls
before me, an invitation, surrounded
on either side by blue baptisia, purple
coneflowers and orange butterfly weed.
Ahead, a hint of sparkling blue trickles
down a rise, catching my eye. The path
becomes a boardwalk through curving,
shiny blue puddles reflecting sun and sky.
Butterflies and bees swoop by.

As I draw nearer, the wet undulating
forms become small round tribute tiles
packed together like a crowd of faces,
honoring our community's women.
Descriptive phrases are etched
on each named clay piece:
"music in friendship,"
"work your passions,"
"poet, gardener, soulmate."

I warm at the sight.
Their lights burn brightly here,
a gathering of stars forming
a constellation we can orbit
forever.

About the Author

Anne Randolph lives in Yellow Springs, Ohio, where she tends a wildflower meadow and a wild backyard. Daily she enjoys nature's gifts, which inspire her poetry. A dedicated conservationist, she has served on boards of land preservation non-profits, including Tecumseh Land Trust and the Arc of Appalachia.

Randolph's poetry has appeared in *Cloudbank, Snowy Egret, Tiny Seed Literary Journal, Mock Turtle Zine,* and *The Listening Eye,* among other journals. Her chapbook *Growing in Light* was published in 2018 by Presa Press. She is helping to edit and organize a winter solstice collection of poetry featuring regional poets, to be published in 2022. She is a member of the Yellow Springs Poetry Group.

www.ingramcontent.com/pod-product-compliance
Lightning Source LLC
Chambersburg PA
CBHW071012160426
43193CB00012B/2025